This book belongs to

____

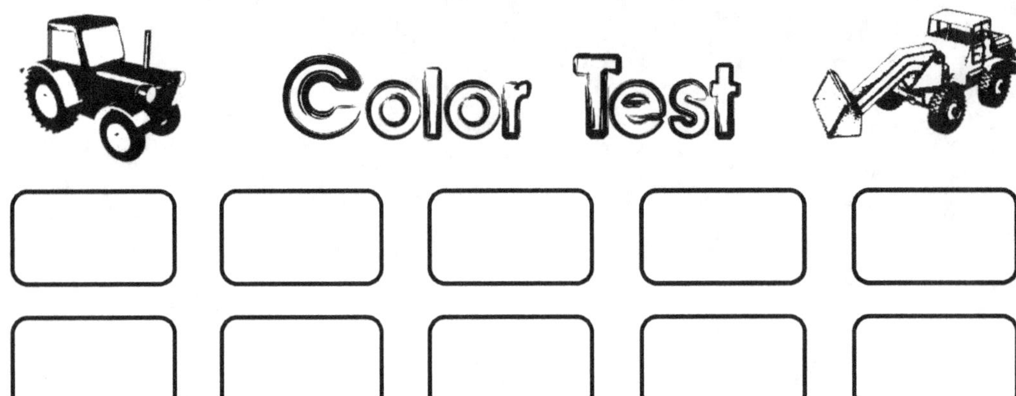

Color Test

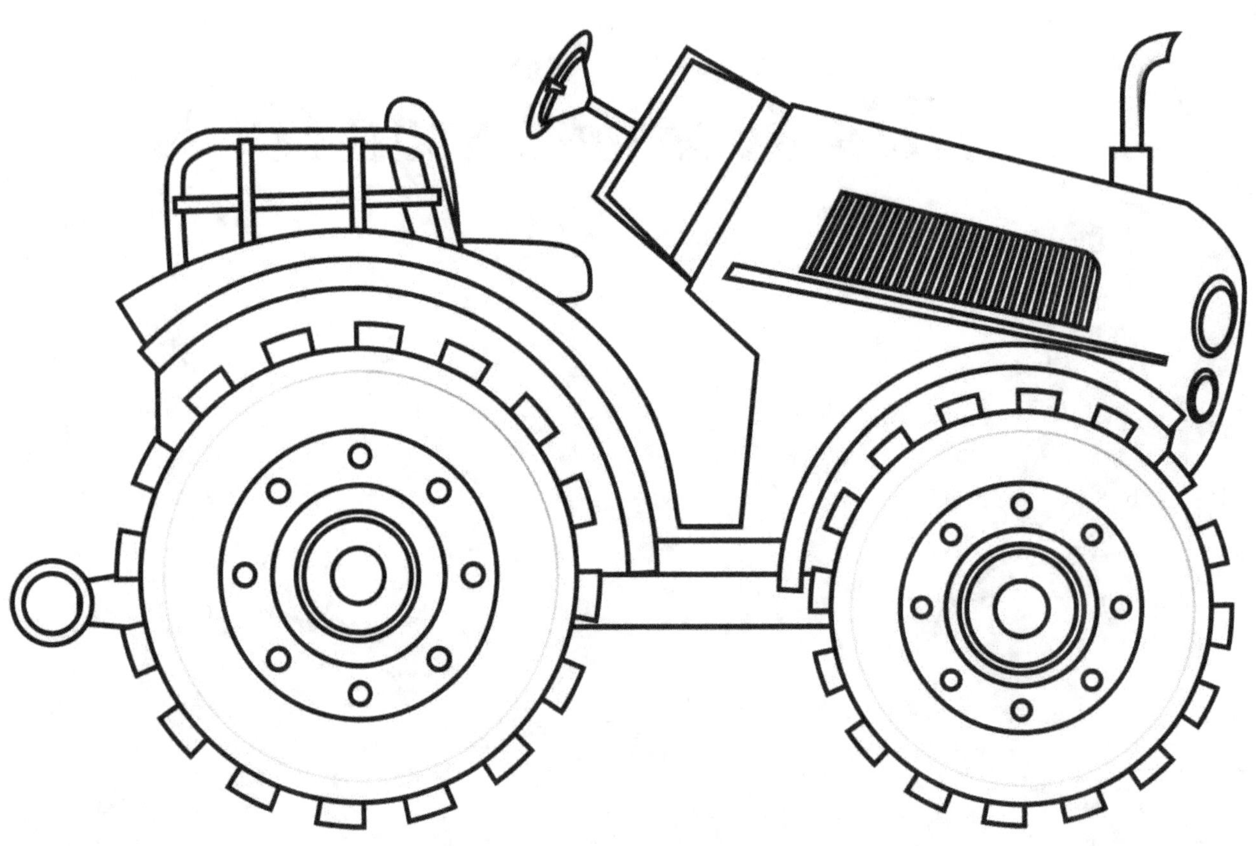

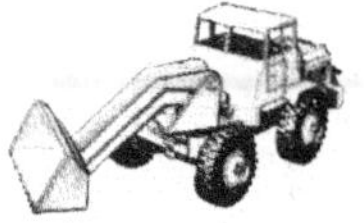

NOW YOU CAN FREELY DRAW AND COLOR YOUR TRACTOR

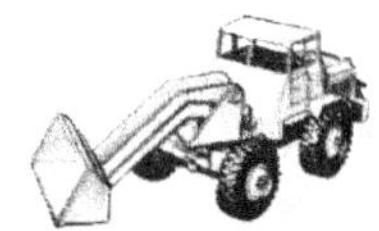

Color Test

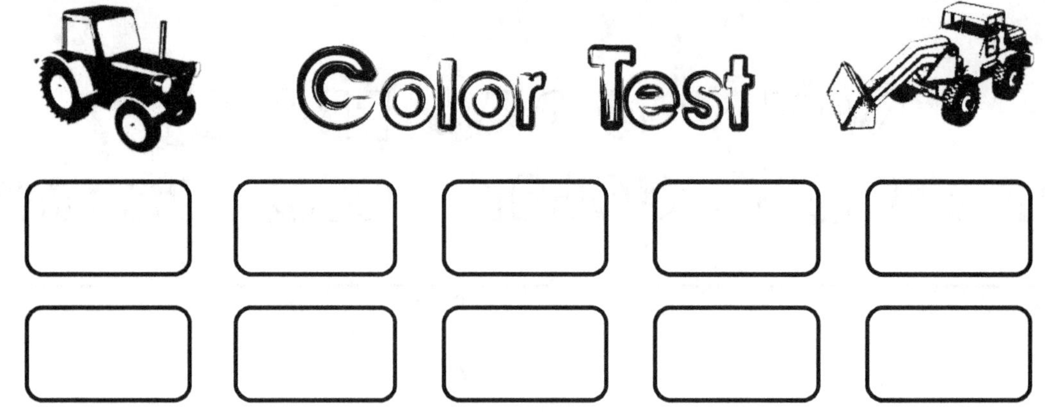

NOW YOU CAN FREELY DRAW AND COLOR YOUR TRACTOR

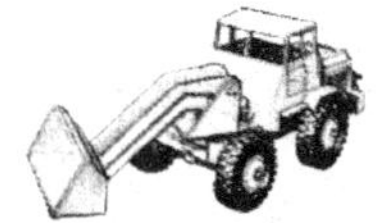

Color Test

NOW YOU CAN FREELY DRAW AND COLOR YOUR TRACTOR

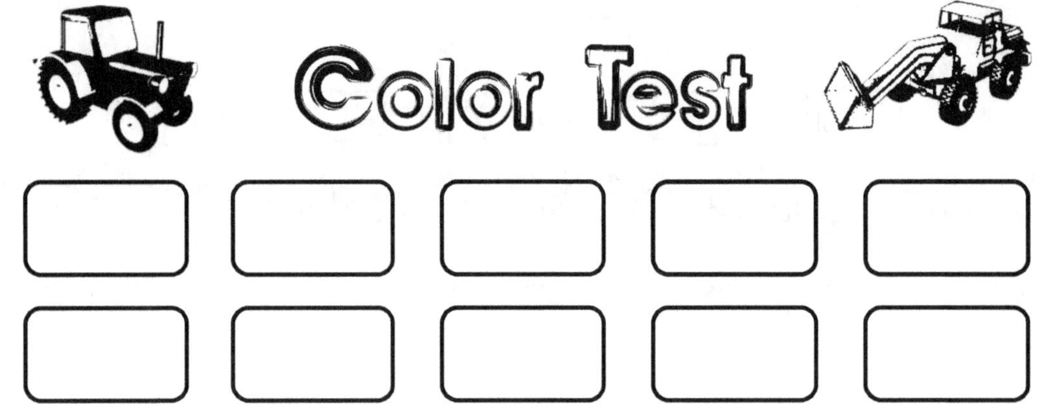

Color Test

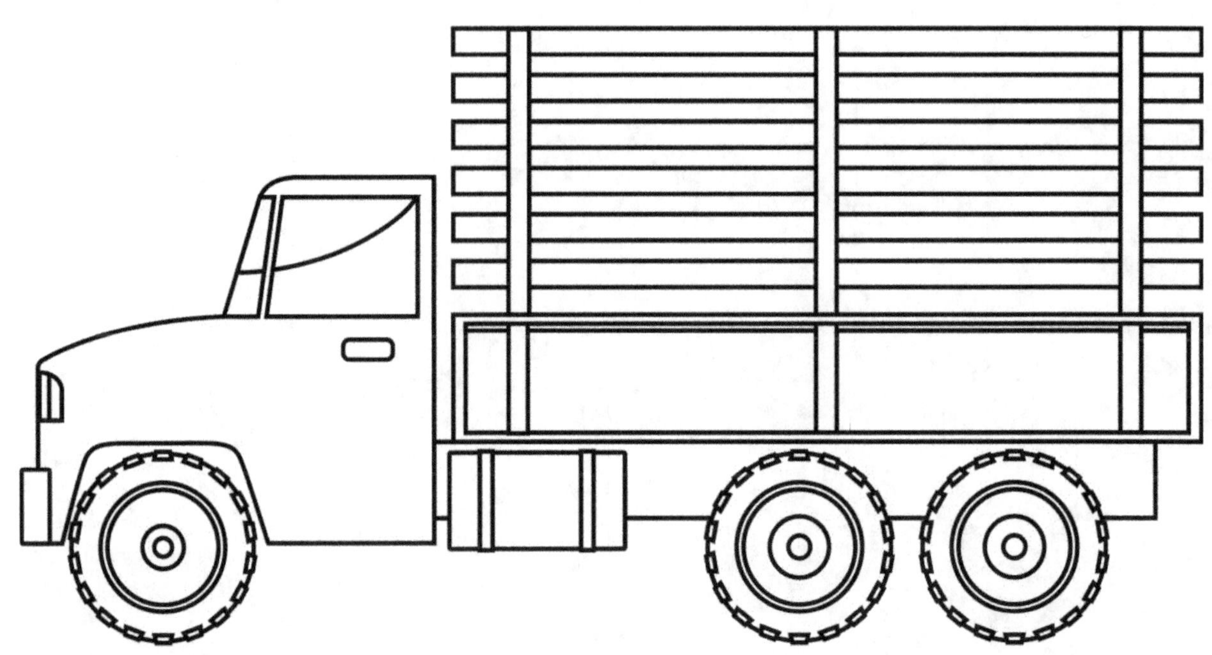

NOW YOU CAN FREELY DRAW AND COLOR YOUR TRACTOR

Color Test

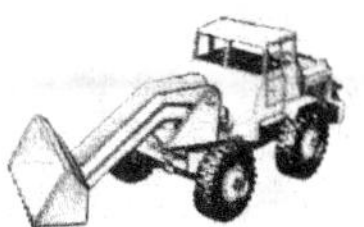

NOW YOU CAN FREELY
DRAW AND COLOR YOUR TRACTOR

Color Test

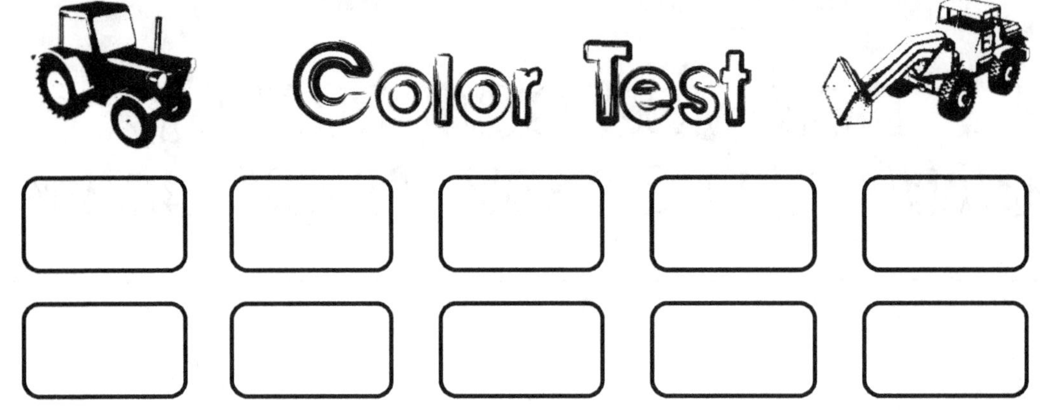

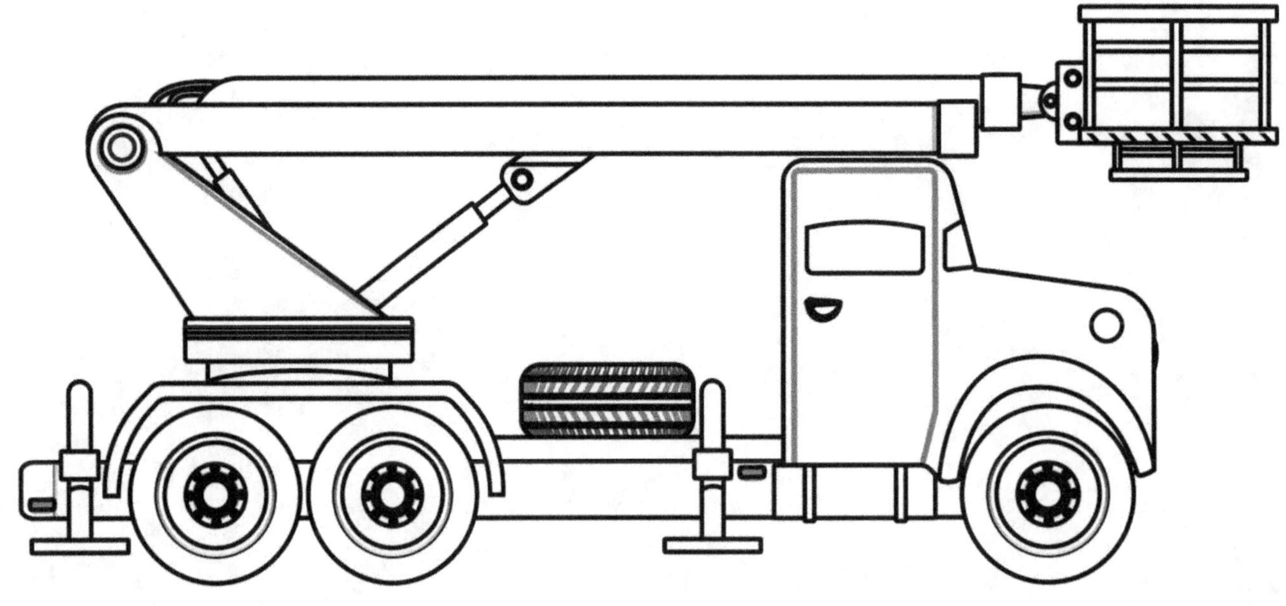

NOW YOU CAN FREELY
DRAW AND COLOR YOUR TRACTOR

Color Test

NOW YOU CAN FREELY
DRAW AND COLOR YOUR TRACTOR

Color Test

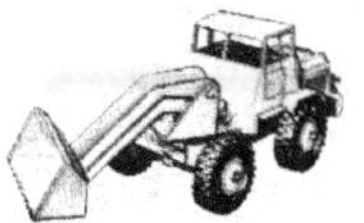

NOW YOU CAN FREELY DRAW AND COLOR YOUR TRACTOR

Color Test

NOW YOU CAN FREELY DRAW AND COLOR YOUR TRACTOR

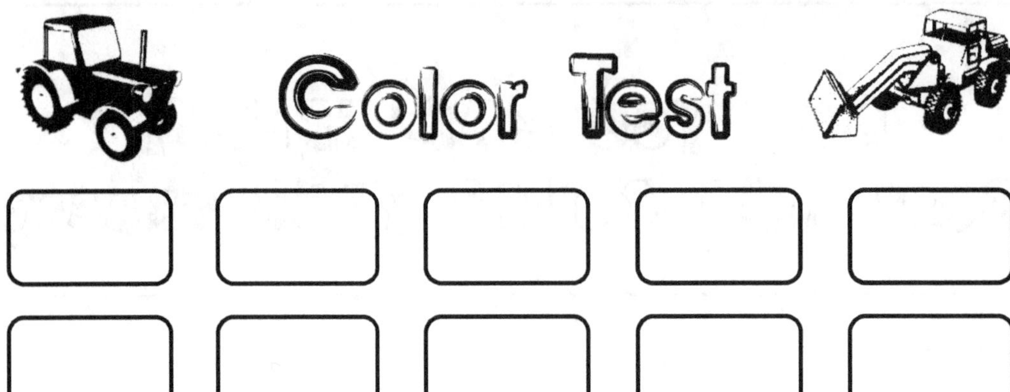

Color Test

NOW YOU CAN FREELY DRAW AND COLOR YOUR TRACTOR

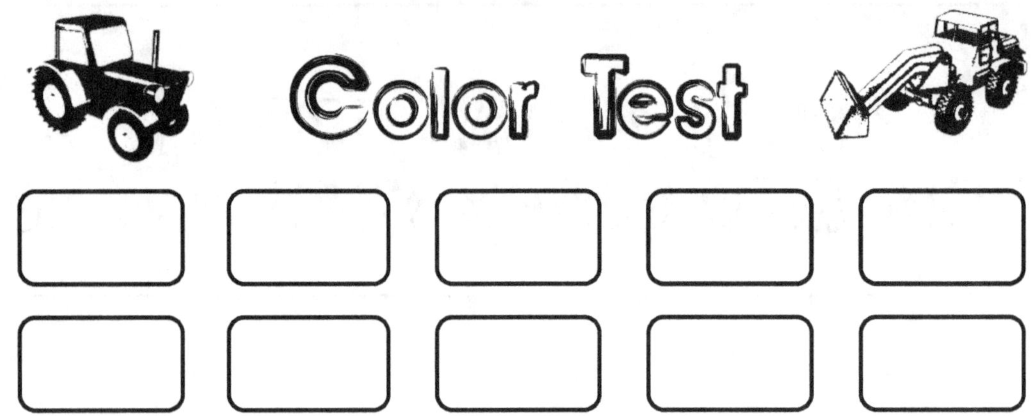

Color Test

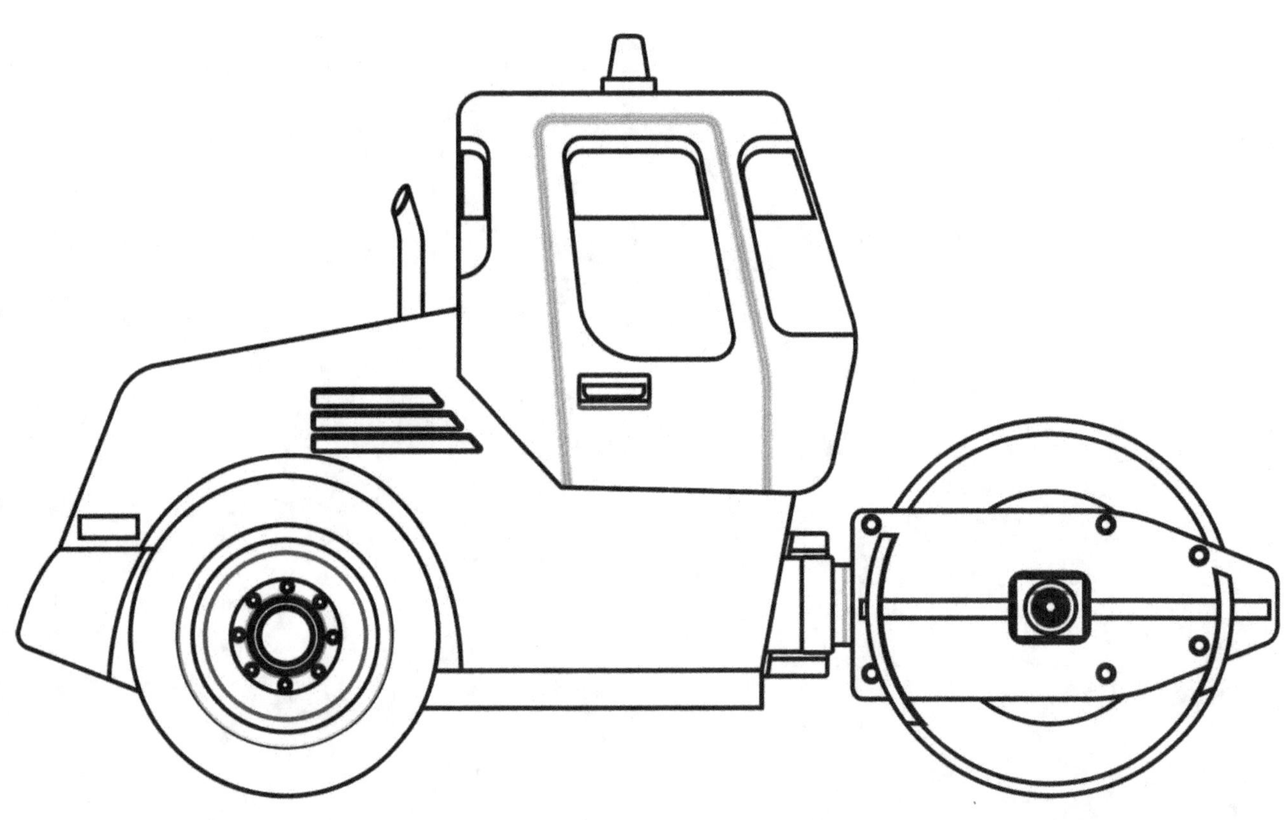

NOW YOU CAN FREELY DRAW AND COLOR YOUR TRACTOR

Color Test

NOW YOU CAN FREELY DRAW AND COLOR YOUR TRACTOR

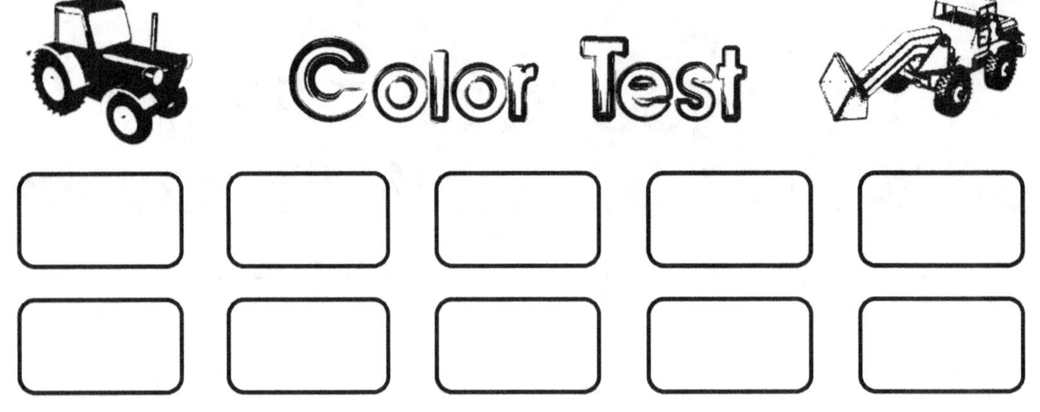

Color Test

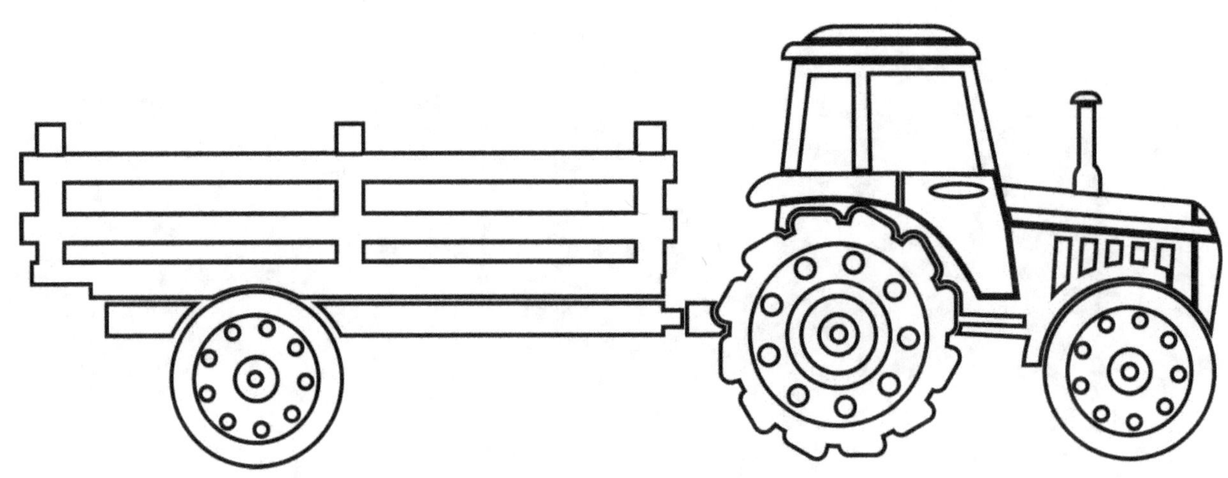

NOW YOU CAN FREELY DRAW AND COLOR YOUR TRACTOR

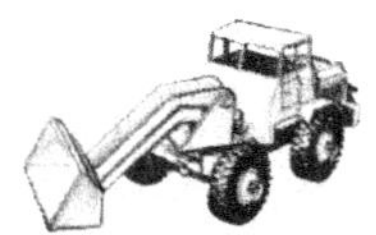

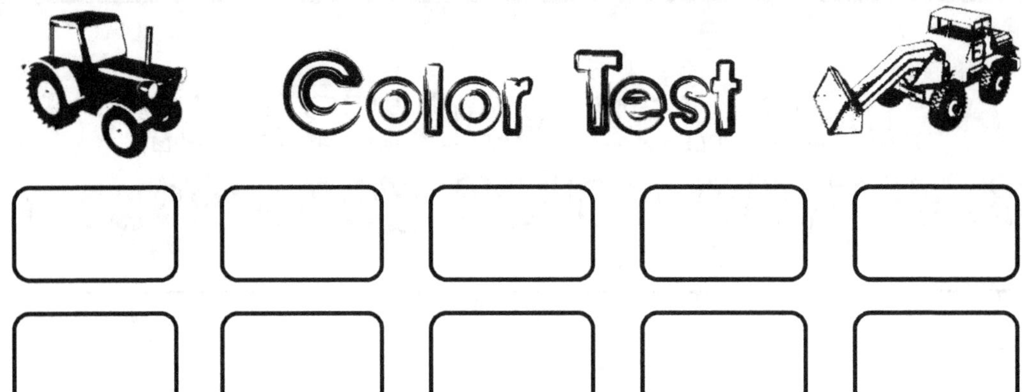

Color Test

NOW YOU CAN FREELY DRAW AND COLOR YOUR TRACTOR

Color Test

NOW YOU CAN FREELY DRAW AND COLOR YOUR TRACTOR

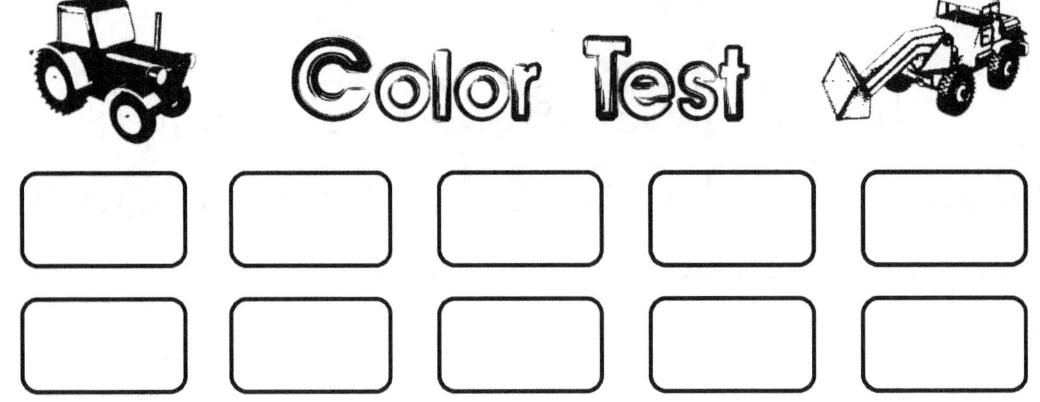

Color Test

NOW YOU CAN FREELY DRAW AND COLOR YOUR TRACTOR

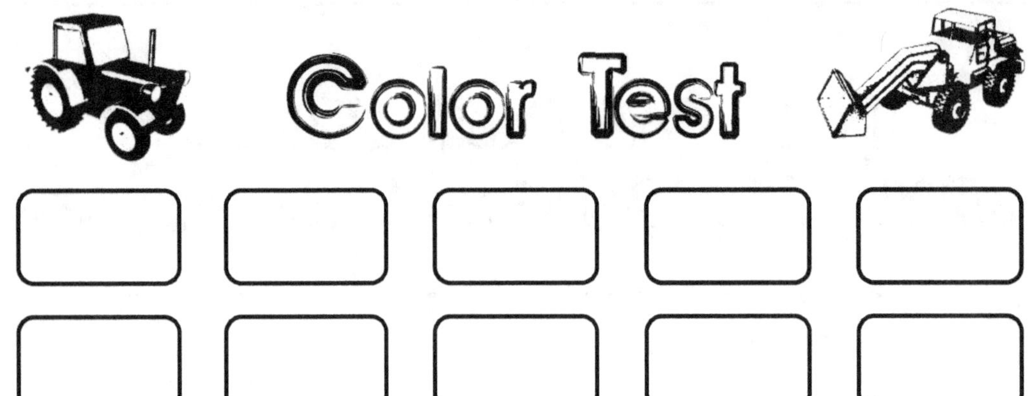

Color Test

NOW YOU CAN FREELY
DRAW AND COLOR YOUR TRACTOR

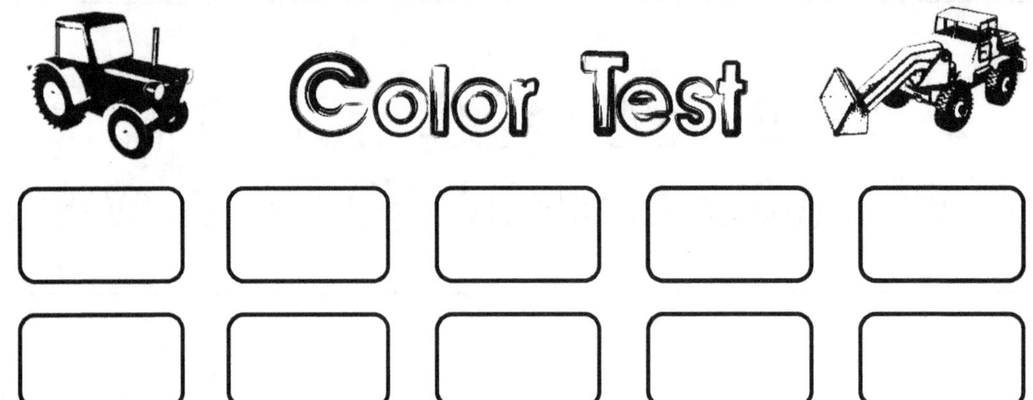

Color Test

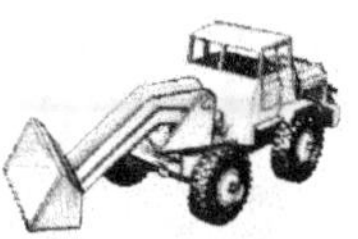

NOW YOU CAN FREELY DRAW AND COLOR YOUR TRACTOR

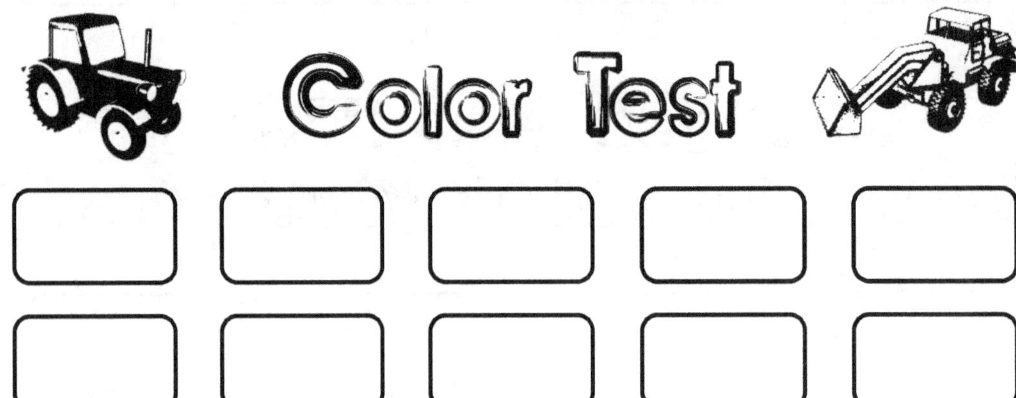

Color Test

NOW YOU CAN FREELY DRAW AND COLOR YOUR TRACTOR

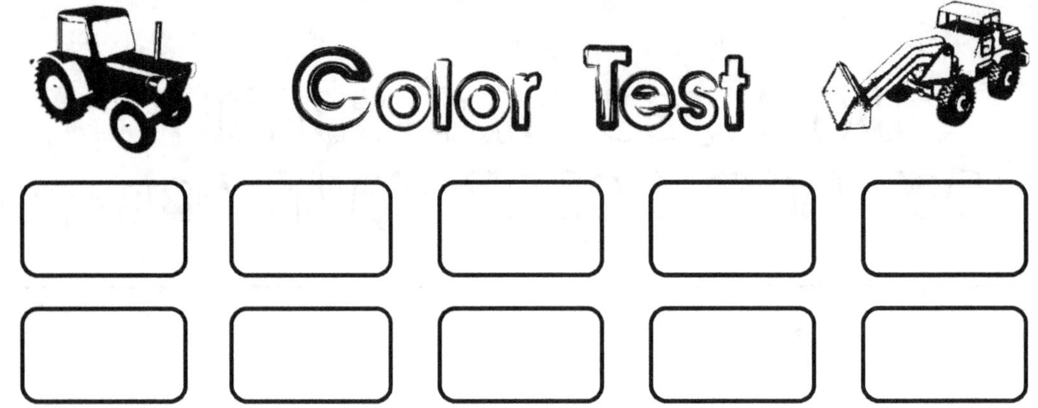

Color Test

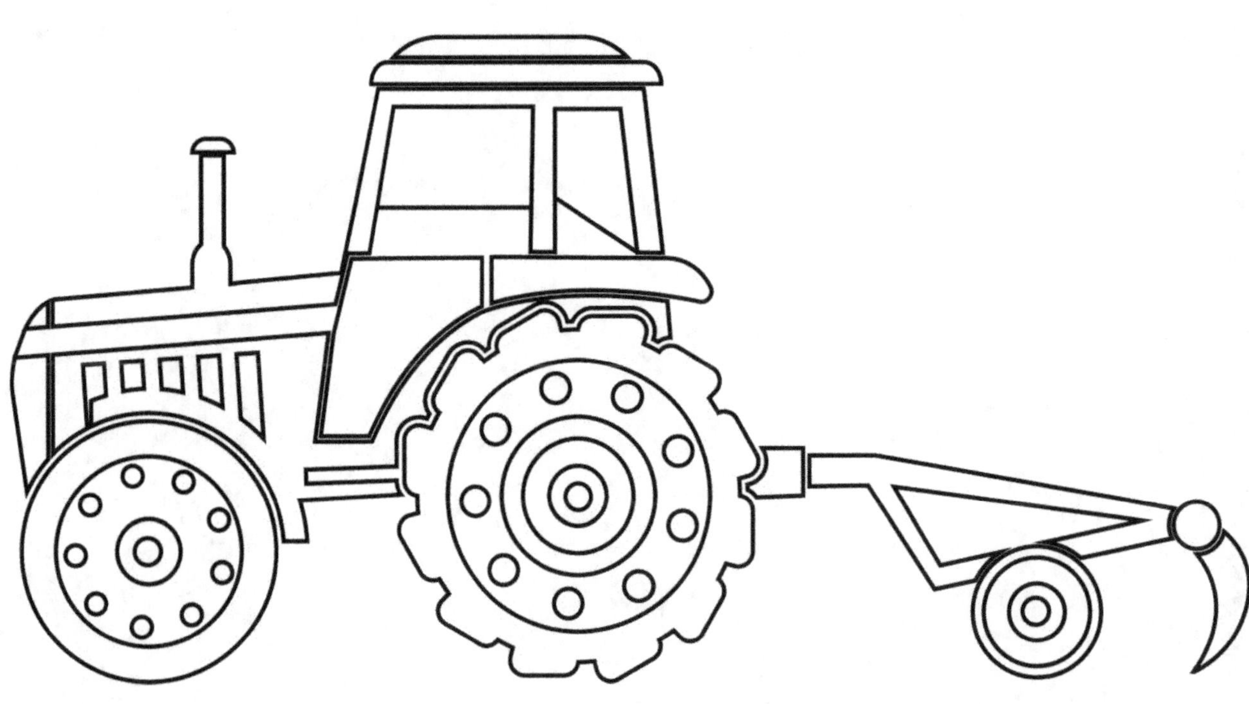

NOW YOU CAN FREELY
DRAW AND COLOR YOUR TRACTOR

Color Test

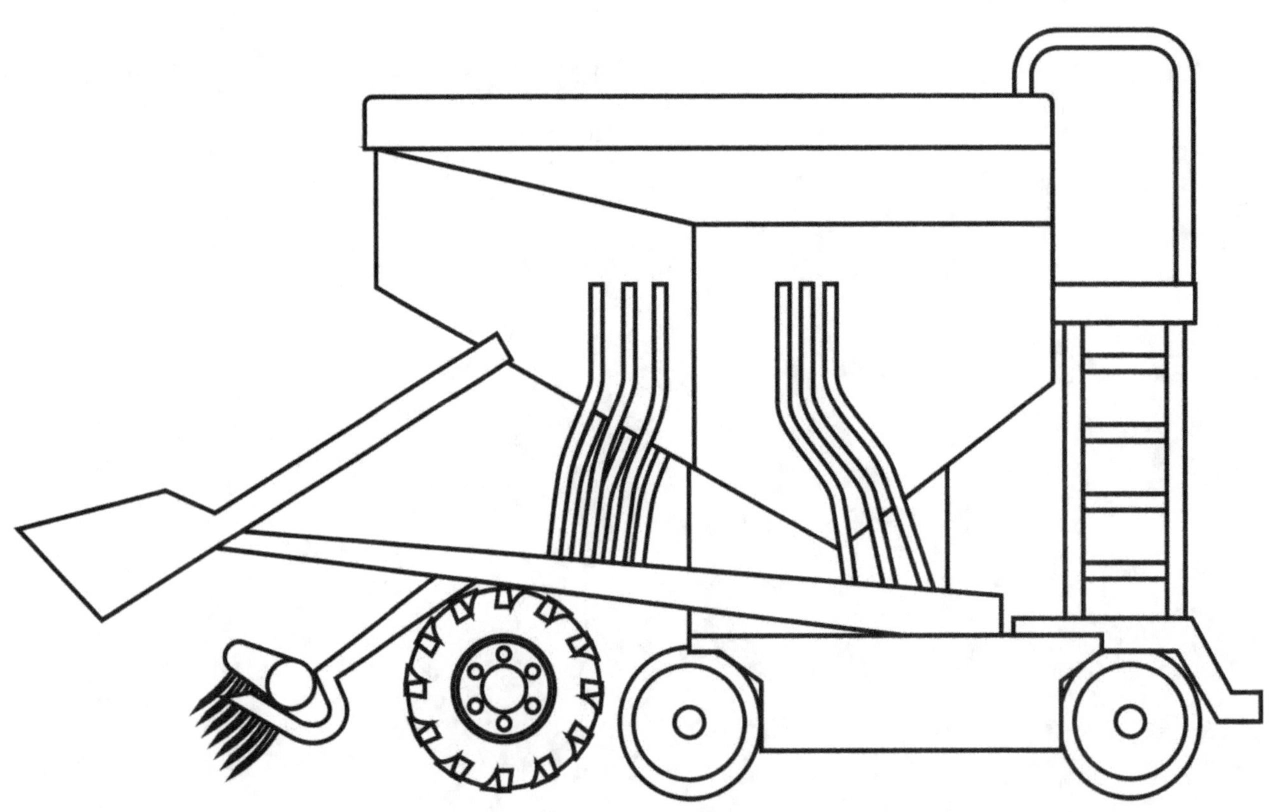

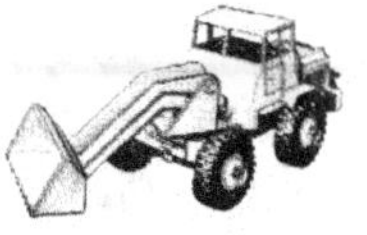

NOW YOU CAN FREELY
DRAW AND COLOR YOUR TRACTOR

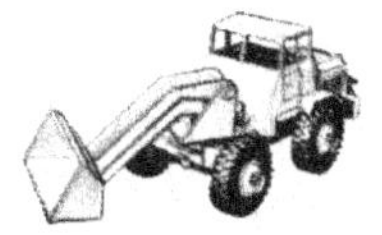

Color Test

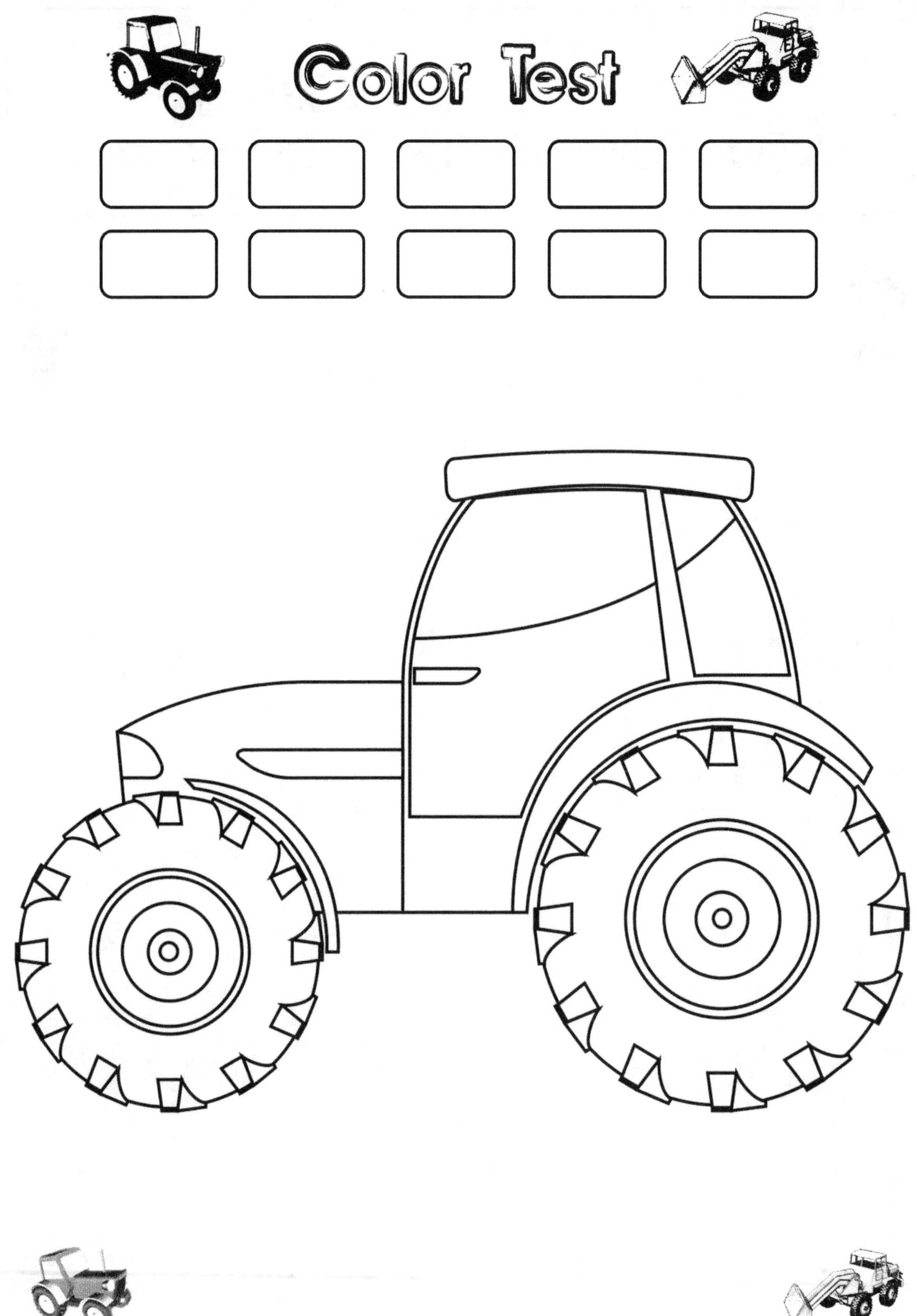

NOW YOU CAN FREELY DRAW AND COLOR YOUR TRACTOR

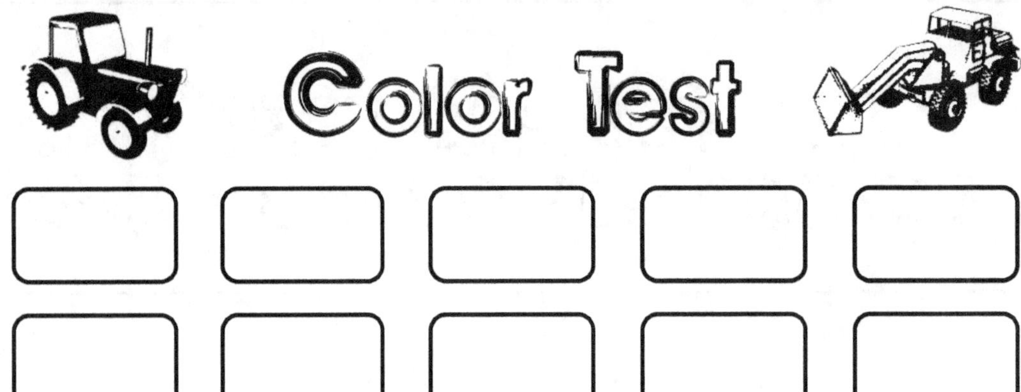

Color Test

NOW YOU CAN FREELY DRAW AND COLOR YOUR TRACTOR

Color Test

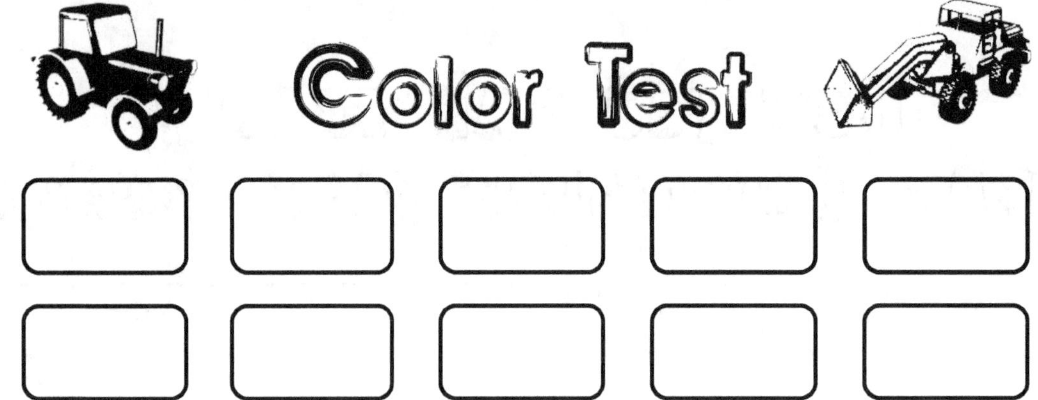

NOW YOU CAN FREELY DRAW AND COLOR YOUR TRACTOR

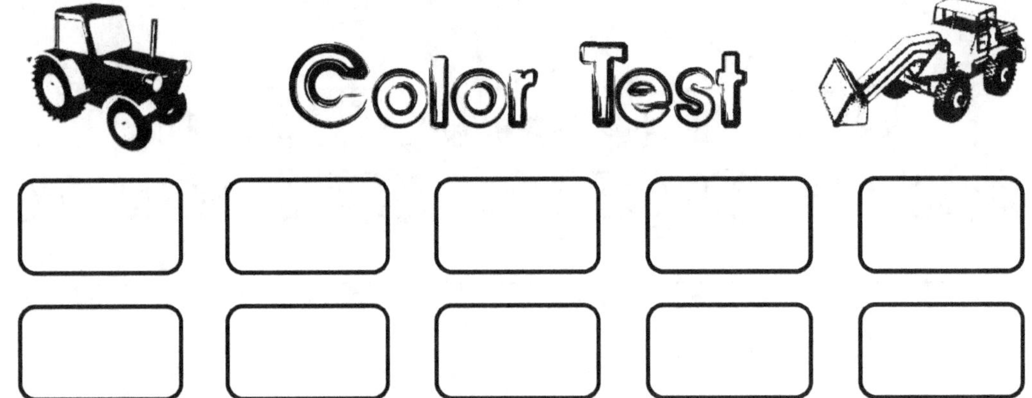

Color Test

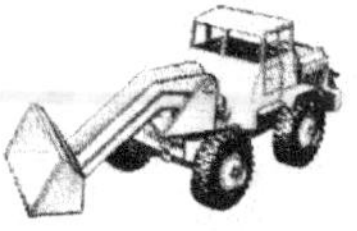

NOW YOU CAN FREELY
DRAW AND COLOR YOUR TRACTOR

Color Test

NOW YOU CAN FREELY DRAW AND COLOR YOUR TRACTOR

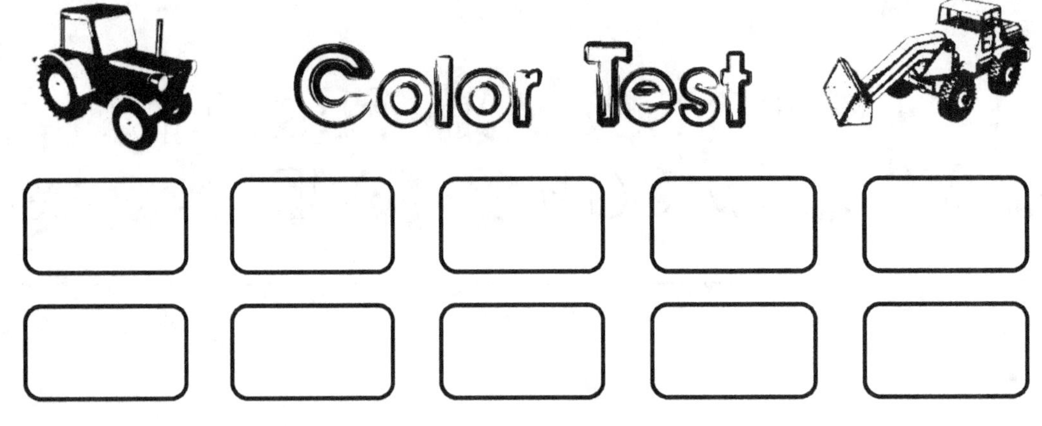

Color Test

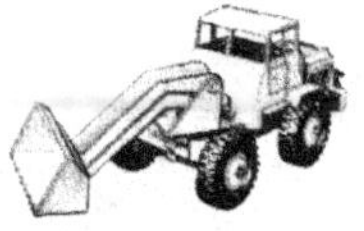

NOW YOU CAN FREELY DRAW AND COLOR YOUR TRACTOR

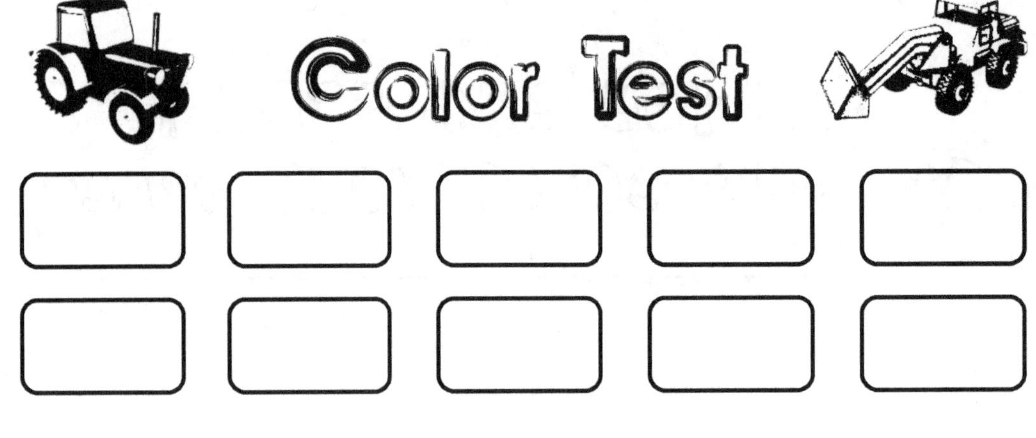

Color Test

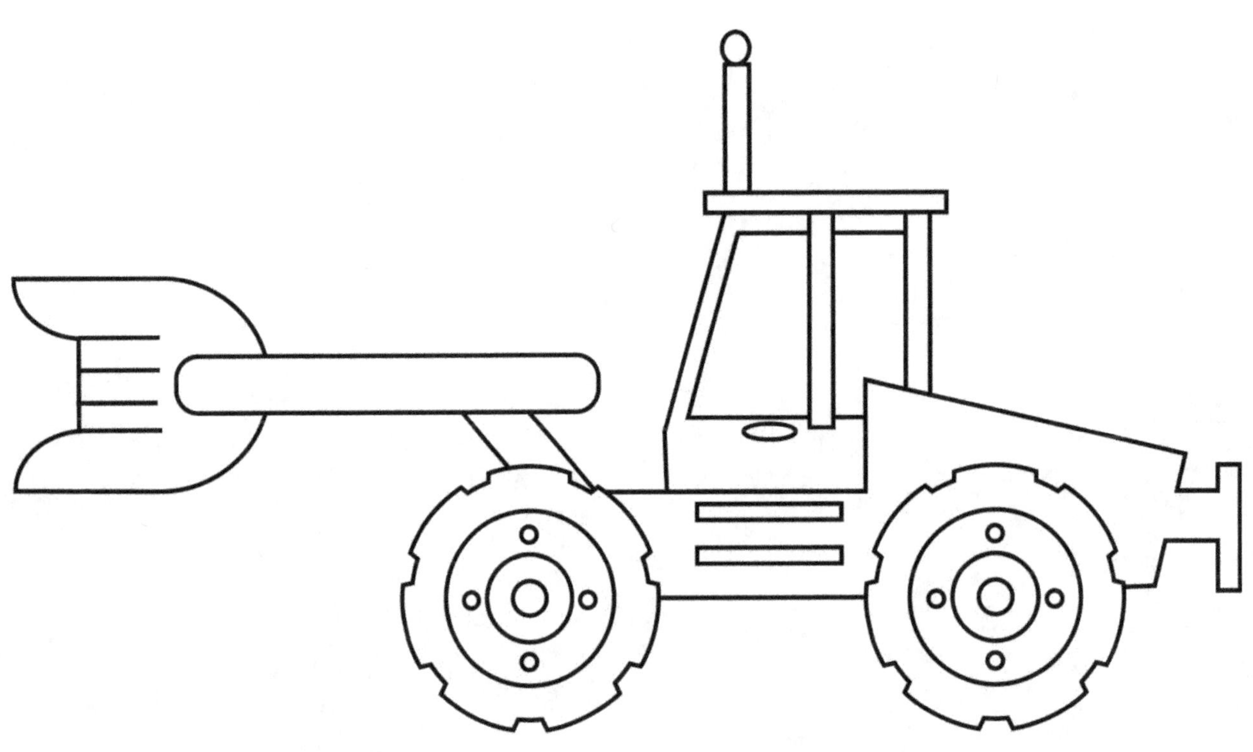

NOW YOU CAN FREELY DRAW AND COLOR YOUR TRACTOR

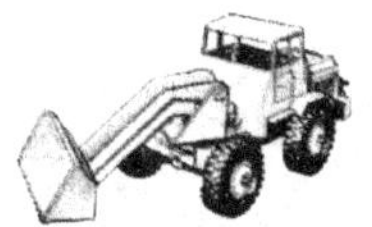

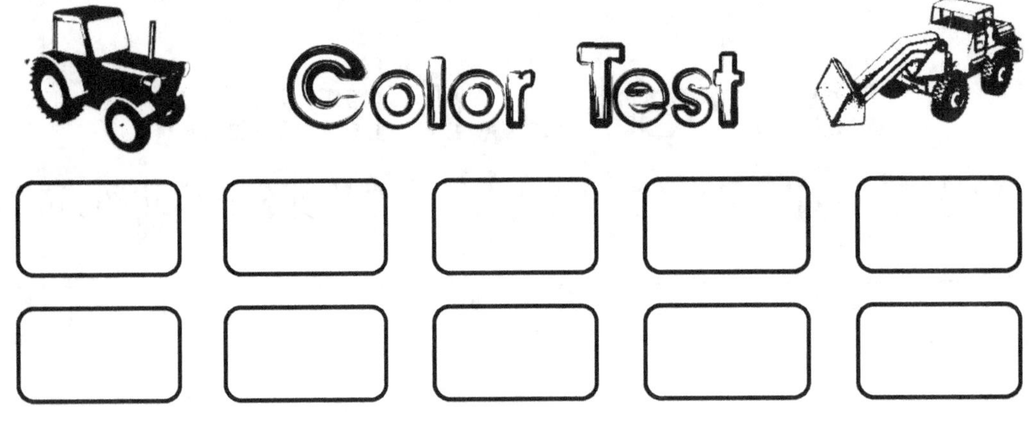
Color Test

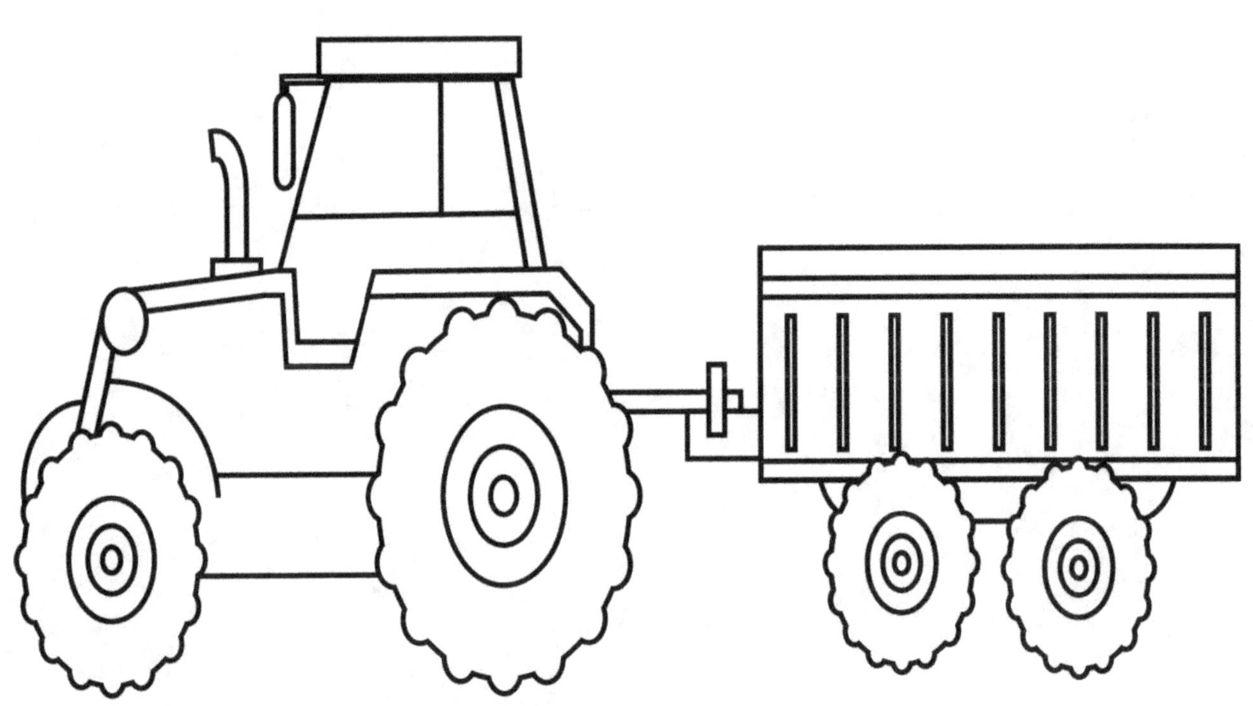

NOW YOU CAN FREELY DRAW AND COLOR YOUR TRACTOR

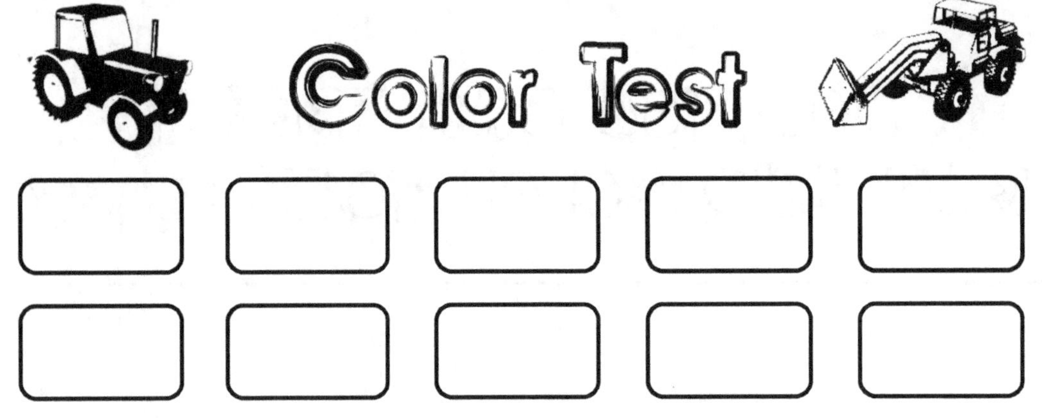

Color Test

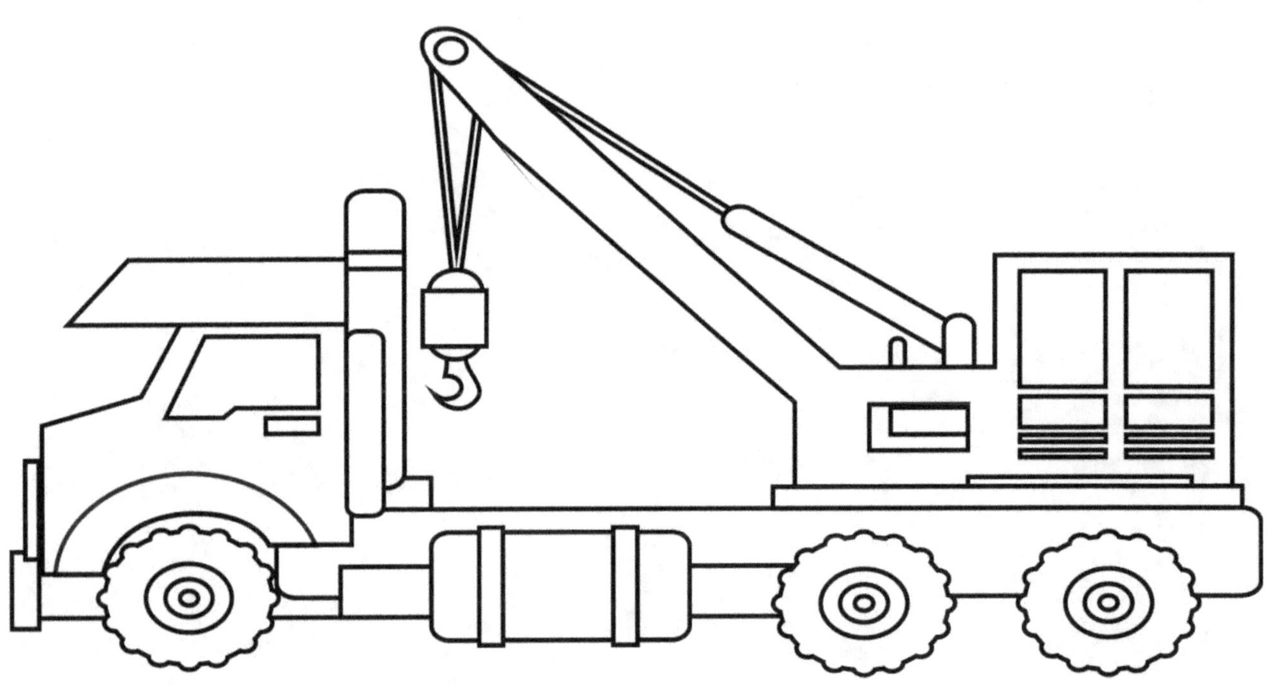

NOW YOU CAN FREELY
DRAW AND COLOR YOUR TRACTOR

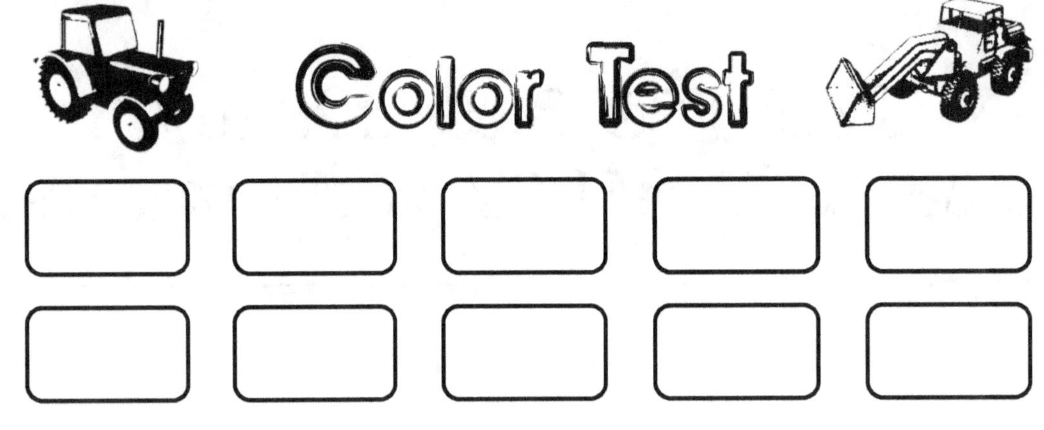
Color Test

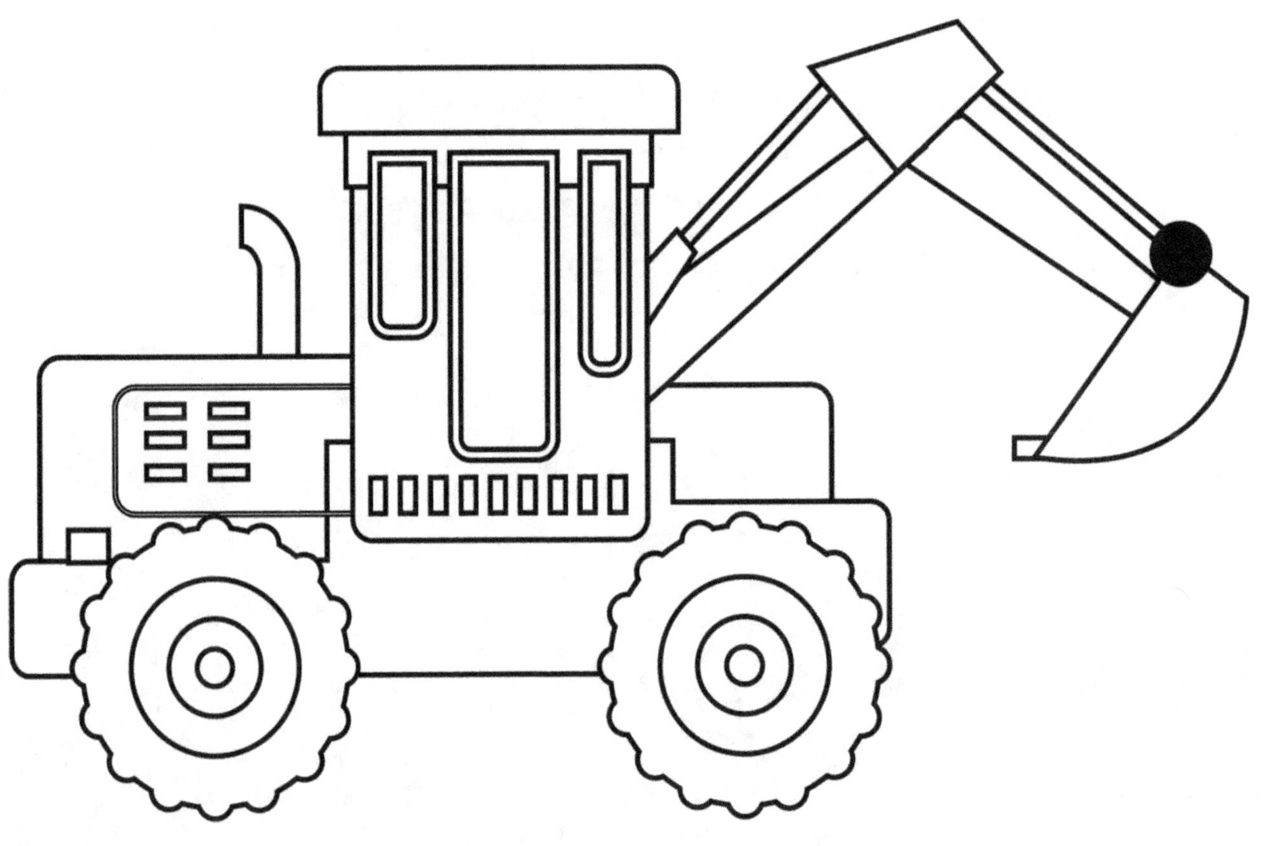

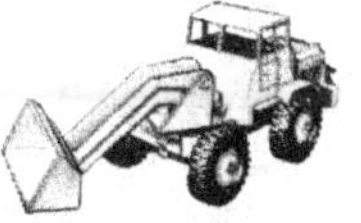

NOW YOU CAN FREELY DRAW AND COLOR YOUR TRACTOR

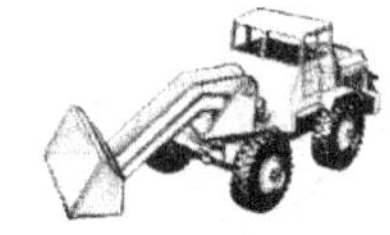

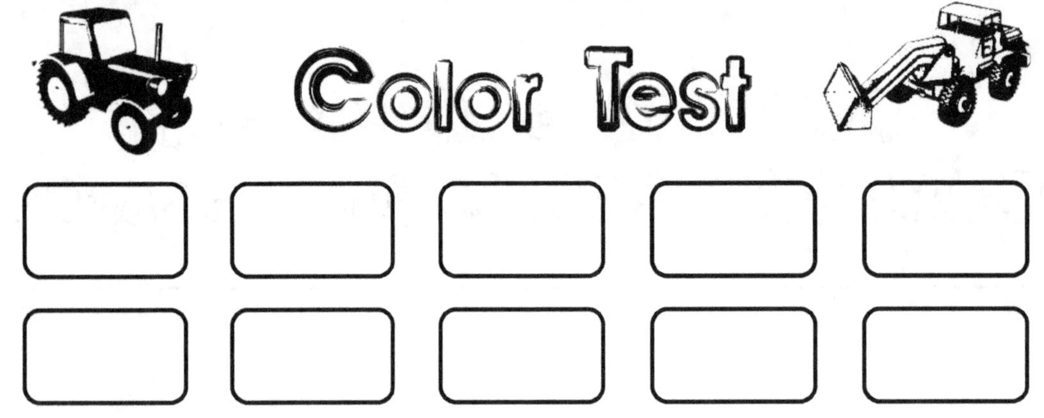

Color Test

NOW YOU CAN FREELY DRAW AND COLOR YOUR TRACTOR

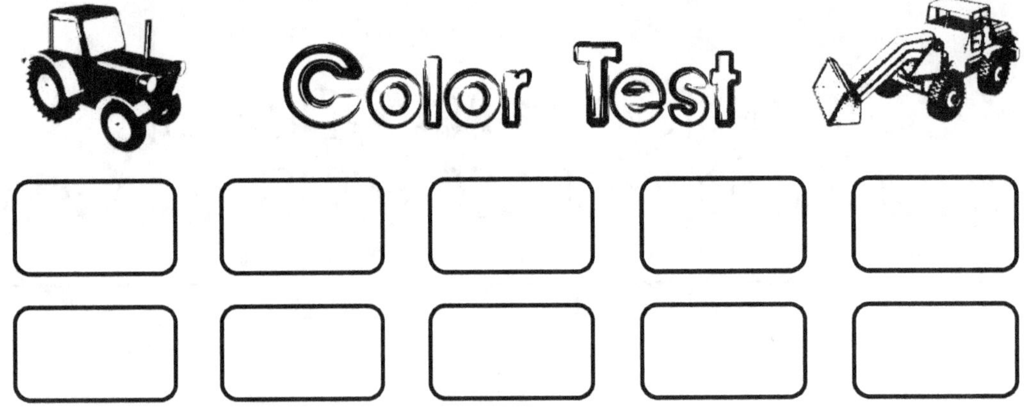

Color Test

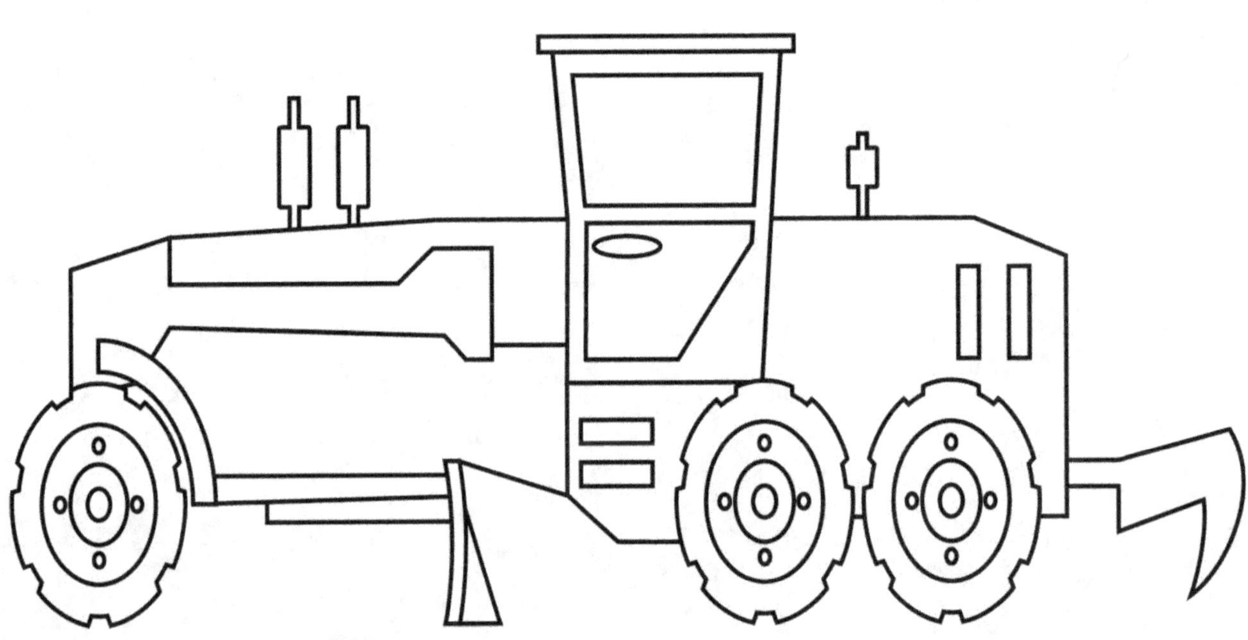

NOW YOU CAN FREELY DRAW AND COLOR YOUR TRACTOR

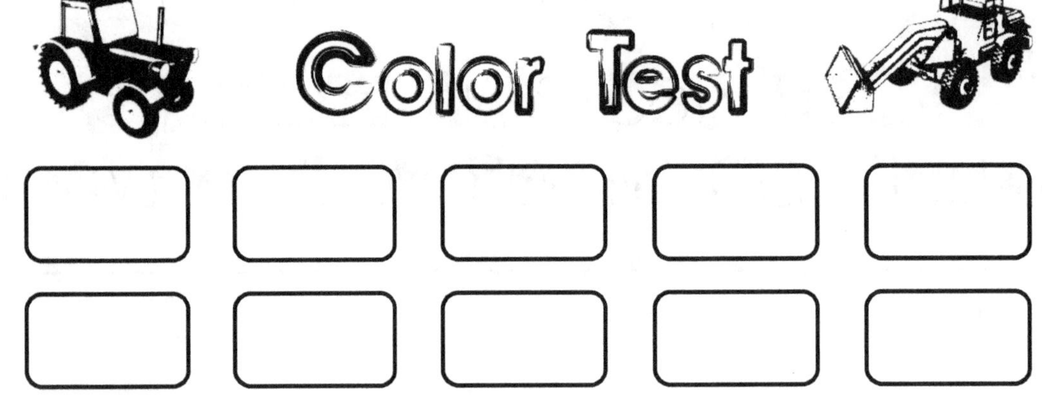

Color Test

NOW YOU CAN FREELY
DRAW AND COLOR YOUR TRACTOR

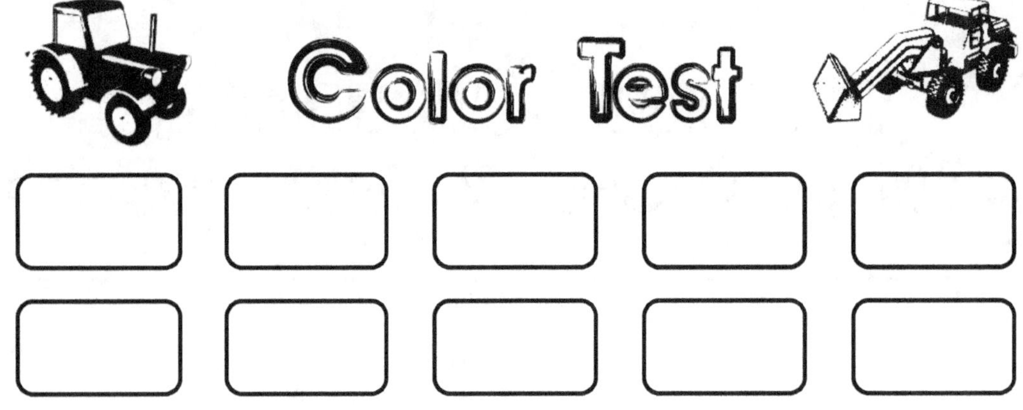

Color Test

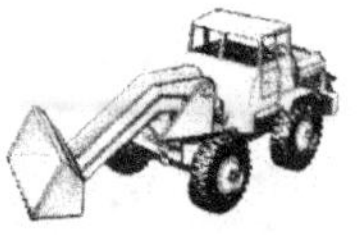

NOW YOU CAN FREELY DRAW AND COLOR YOUR TRACTOR

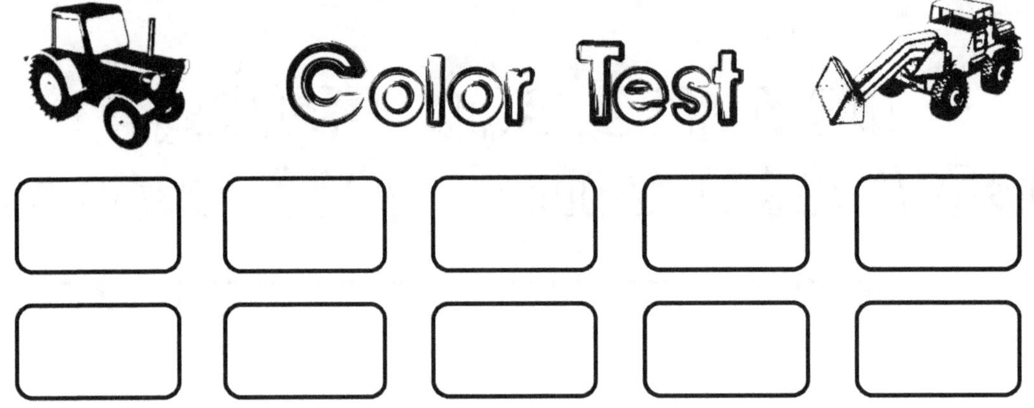

Color Test

NOW YOU CAN FREELY DRAW AND COLOR YOUR TRACTOR

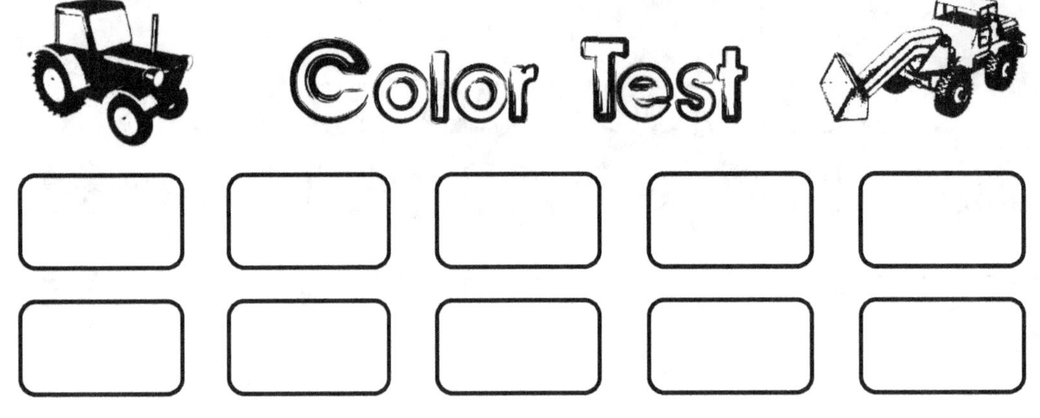

Color Test

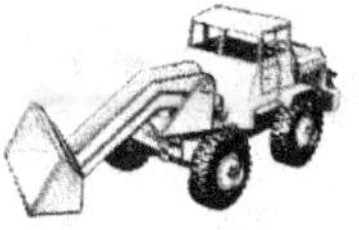

NOW YOU CAN FREELY DRAW AND COLOR YOUR TRACTOR

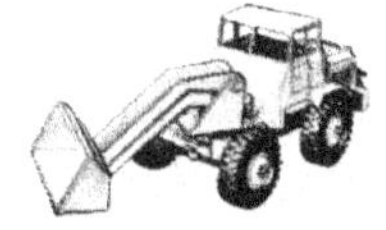

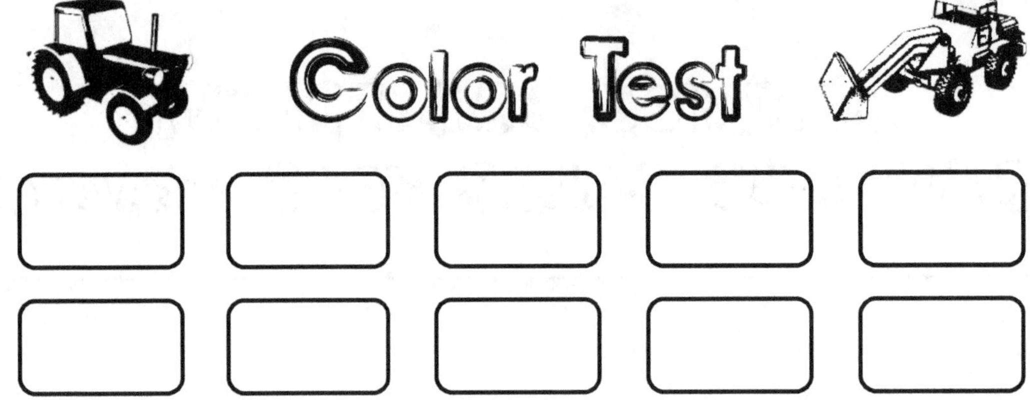

Color Test

NOW YOU CAN FREELY
DRAW AND COLOR YOUR TRACTOR

Color Test

NOW YOU CAN FREELY DRAW AND COLOR YOUR TRACTOR